CW00351444

Top Tips for PET

Acknowledgements

For permission to reproduce photographs:

Photolibrary for p. 52

Cambridge ESOL would also like to thank the following for their contributions to this project:

Sharon Ashton, Annette Capel, Helen Naylor.

University of Cambridge ESOL Examinations
1 Hills Road, Cambridge, CB1 2EU, UK
www.CambridgeESOL.org

© UCLES 2009

First published 2009
Printed in the United Kingdom by Océ (UK) Ltd

ISBN: 978-1-906438-50-0

Contents

Introduction

Top Tips for PET is an essential part of your revision for the Preliminary English Test (PET), the B1-level exam from Cambridge ESOL. Each of the three main chapters (Reading and Writing, Listening and Speaking) follows the same structure and is based on a series of pieces of advice (the 'tips') which examiners have collected from many years' experience of writing and marking PET papers.

Each section usually starts with a tip at the top of the page. The tip is followed by an example taken from real PET material and a clear explanation to help you understand exactly what it means.

Each chapter ends with some more 'General tips'. There is also a handy section at the beginning of the book on how to revise for PET and a very important section at the back on what you should do on the day of the exam.

How to use *Top Tips for PET*

Take the *Top Tips for PET* book with you and read it when you have a few minutes during the day. Then use the CD-ROM to practise at home: it contains a real interactive PET exam for you to try, together with the answers and some feedback for Reading and Listening and some sample student answers for the Writing paper. The CD-ROM also includes all the recordings for the Listening paper and a video of real students doing a PET Speaking test, to show you exactly what you will have to do when you take the test. Practise with some classmates using the Speaking test material on the CD-ROM and compare your performance with the students on the video.

Top Tips for PET is flexible. You can look at a different tip from a different paper every day, or you can start at the beginning with the tips for the Reading and Writing paper and work through until you get to the end of the tips for the Speaking test. Whichever method you prefer, read the example and the explanation carefully to make sure that you understand each tip. When you have understood all the tips for each paper, try the real exam on the CD-ROM.

Guide to symbols

 This symbol introduces the 'tip' which is usually at the top of the page. Each tip is some useful advice to help you find the right answer for Reading or Listening. For Writing, the tips show you how to write a better answer to the question, and for Speaking, they explain how you can give good answers which show your true level of English to the examiners.

 This is an extra piece of advice which is important for a particular part of the test.

 This symbol tells you to go to the CD-ROM, where you will find a real PET exam to try.

We hope that *Top Tips for PET* will help you with your preparation for taking the PET exam.

Cambridge ESOL

Guide to PET task types

Multiple choice You have to read a text or listen to a recording. Each question has three or four options and you have to decide which the correct answer is. *(Reading: Parts 1, 4 and 5 and Listening: Parts 1 and 2)*

Matching You read a series of descriptions and several short texts. For each question, you have to decide which text is most suitable for each description. *(Reading: Part 2)*

True/false You have to read a text or listen to a recording and decide if statements in a list are correct or incorrect. *(Reading: Part 3 and Listening: Part 4)*

Cloze You read a text in which there are some missing words or phrases (gaps). *(Reading: Part 5)*

Sentence transformation You have to complete a sentence so that it has exactly the same meaning as the first sentence you are given. *(Writing: Part 1)*

Guided writing You are told what to write about in a short message such as an email. It is important that you write about each point that is indicated. *(Writing: Part 2)*

Extended writing You have to write a longer piece of writing: you choose from either a letter to a friend or a story. *(Writing: Part 3)*

Gap-fill While you listen to a recording, you complete the sentences or notes with the information that you hear. There are empty spaces (gaps) in the notes or sentences that you have to fill in. *(Listening: Part 3)*

Collaborative task The examiner gives you a picture and a decision-making task to do. You have to talk with the other candidate and make a decision. *(Speaking: Part 2)*

Long turn The examiner gives you a photograph to talk about and you have to speak for about 1 minute without interruption. *(Speaking: Part 3)*

How to revise for PET

It is important to use the time that you have to revise for PET as well as possible. Here are some general ideas to help you do this.

Make a plan

It is a good idea to make a plan for your last month's study before the exam. Think about:

- what you need to do
- how much time you have
- how you can fit what you need to do into that time.

Try to be realistic when you make your plan. If you plan to do too much, then you may soon be disappointed when you fall behind.

Think about what you need to know

Remember that PET is a test of your general level of English. You don't have an exam syllabus listing what information you have to learn as you do in, for example, chemistry or history. So most things that you do in English will help you to improve – reading a story or reading something in English on the internet may be as useful as doing a grammar exercise, for example.

It is important, however, that you know exactly what you will have to do in the exam. Doing some practice papers will help you develop good exam techniques and this will save you time in the exam room. But don't spend all your revision time doing practice papers!

Think about what you need to improve. Ask your English teacher what you need to work on – reading, writing, speaking or listening, grammar or vocabulary.

Look back at homework that your teacher has corrected. What mistakes did you make? Do you understand where you went wrong? What are your weaknesses?

Have what you need to hand

In order to prepare for PET you probably need:

- a good learners' dictionary (one with examples of how words are actually used in English)
- a PET-level coursebook (you are probably using one of these if you do regular classes)
- some examples of PET papers
- a vocabulary notebook
- notes or other materials from your English course (if you are doing one)
- a bilingual dictionary
- a good grammar book.

If you have access to a computer you can get some of these online – the dictionaries and the examples of PET papers, for instance.

Make sure you have the stationery you need, such as pens, pencils and paper. Some students also find it helpful to write things like vocabulary on cards, which they then carry with them and look at when they are on the bus or in a café.

Think about when and where you study

Most people find it best to study at regular times at a desk with a good light and everything they need beside them.

Some people find they work best in the early mornings while others prefer the evenings. If possible, do most of your revision at the time of day which is best for you.

However, you may also find that there are other good times and places for you to study. Perhaps when you are with friends at the weekend you could watch a DVD in English. Or you could read an English magazine during your journey to school.

Organise your revision time well

Allow time for breaks when you are revising – many students like to study for an hour and a half, for example, and then have a half-hour break.

Vary what you do – sometimes focus on listening, sometimes on vocabulary, sometimes on writing. This will help you to look at various aspects of the language and it will also make your revision more interesting.

It is important to have some time when you forget about revision. You cannot study every minute of the day – go out and see your friends, do some sport, go to the cinema or read a book.

Enjoy your revision!

Find some enjoyable activities that help your English – listen to songs in English or watch TV or some English-language DVDs.

What do you like doing in your free time? Could you combine that with English practice too? For example, if you like a particular sport or singer or if you are interested in computer games, you should easily be able to find something in English about your interest on the internet.

Revise with a friend – you can practise talking to each other in English and can perhaps help each other with any questions you have.

Keep fit!

Don't forget that feeling fit and healthy will help you get good marks too:

- make sure you get enough sleep
- remember to eat well
- take some exercise.

Now here are some ideas to help you organise your revision for the individual papers in PET.

Paper 1: Reading

The more you read in English before the exam, the better you will do in this paper. Reading is probably the best way to improve your grammar and vocabulary.

You will learn most if you enjoy what you are reading. So don't choose something that is too difficult for you. Remember that it doesn't have to be serious – unless, of course, you prefer serious things. There are lots of different students who have enjoyed each of these types of reading:

- newspaper articles
- sports magazines
- film reviews
- romantic stories
- children's stories
- travel information – about your own country or a place you have been to
- translations of books you have already read in your own language
- graded readers (well-known books which are adapted to your level of English).

Don't look up every word in a dictionary when you read as this will stop you enjoying what you read. Just look up the meaning of words that are important for your general understanding. Then when you have finished you can go back and look up some more words and make a note of any useful expressions from the text.

Keep a reading diary – write a couple of sentences in English about what you have read. This should help you to use some of the language from what you have read. It will also help you with the Writing paper.

Paper 1: Writing

For this paper, it is important to practise writing regularly in English.

- For the first part of the Writing paper (the sentence transformation task) you need to have good control of grammar and vocabulary. So, do some extra practice with materials which focus on grammar and vocabulary (your teacher may be able to advise you on which books are best).

- For the second part of the Writing paper, you have to write a short message such as an email or a postcard. The task may ask you to make an apology or a suggestion and it is helpful to practise the language you need for these different functions.
- For the third part of the Writing paper you have to write a letter to a friend or write a story. You will need to think about how you organise a letter and to learn some common phrases for starting and finishing a letter. For the story, you need to think about the structure of stories (reading short stories in English will help) and practise writing stories about specific topics.
- You often learn best when you write or talk about things that are important to you. So practise making sentences about your own life using structures or vocabulary that you want to learn.
- Use some of the new vocabulary and expressions that you have learned from your reading.
- If possible ask a teacher or native English speaker to correct your work. Ask them to correct your mistakes and also to suggest a more interesting way of expressing what you want to say.
- Listen carefully to their advice and use it in the next piece of writing that you do.

Paper 2: Listening

Even if you are a long way from an English-speaking country, it is possible to practise listening to English. For example, there are lots of things you can listen to on the internet.

- Listen to short programmes in English on the radio or on an English-language TV channel as much as possible.
- Watch DVDs of English-language films. You may be able to watch a film with subtitles. This can make listening easier and more enjoyable and will help to give you confidence in listening to English.
- Try watching a film in English that you have already seen in your own language.
- Listen to songs in English. It is often possible to find the words for songs on the internet.

Paper 3: Speaking

Make the effort to practise speaking English whenever you can.

- Get together with friends and agree that you will speak only English for half an hour.
- Join an English-language club if there is one in your area.
- Try to make contact with English speakers visiting your area.
- If there are students whose first language is English in your area, try to arrange to exchange conversation sessions with them. (You talk for half an hour in your language and half an hour in English.)
- Try talking to other English-language speakers on the internet.
- When listening to English-language films or television, think about the language that the speakers use and, where possible, make use of it when you are speaking yourself.
- Make sure that you can talk about yourself, give opinions, ask someone to repeat or explain, agree and disagree. You may need to do all of these things in the exam.

We hope these ideas will help you to make the most of your revision time. Above all, we hope that you enjoy your studies and wish you all the very best for the exam.

Paper 1: Reading and Writing

What's in Reading (Parts 1–5)?

Part 1 ⓠ 5 notices or short texts with 5 multiple-choice questions
☑ 1 mark for each correct answer

Part 2 ⓠ 8 short texts with 5 matching questions
☑ 1 mark for each correct answer

Part 3 ⓠ 1 text with 10 true/false questions
☑ 1 mark for each correct answer

Part 4 ⓠ 1 text with 5 multiple-choice questions
☑ 1 mark for each correct answer

Part 5 ⓠ 1 text with 10 multiple-choice questions
☑ 1 mark for each correct answer

🕐 About **50 minutes**

Reading: Part 1 multiple choice

 TIP: Don't look for the same word in the options and the text. Think of synonyms (words with a similar meaning), then choose the option (A, B or C) that is closest in meaning to the text.

Example

Here is an example of a Part 1 Reading question.

Star Theatre

Coming soon:

The Comedy Show

Book early to avoid disappointment.

(Q)

A Ticket sales for this show have been disappointing and it has been cancelled.

B If you would like to see the show, you should get your tickets as soon as possible.

C Unfortunately, there are no tickets left for the early performance of this show.

Explanation: The highlighted words give you the answer. 'Get your tickets as soon as possible' (option B) is another way of saying 'book early'. It does not mean that the show has been 'cancelled' (option A) or that there are 'no tickets left' (option C). So the answer is **B**.

Reading: Part 1 multiple choice

 TIP: It is important to think about the purpose of the message. This means thinking about why the person has written the message.

Example

Here is an example of a Part 1 Reading question.

FROM: Mum

TO: Susan

When you arrive at the airport give me a ring and I'll come and pick you up. You've got too much luggage to get the train back home.

(Q) **Susan's mother**
A is advising her to be careful with her bags at the airport.
B is explaining why she cannot meet her at the airport.
C is offering to drive her home from the airport.

Explanation: The highlighted words refer to the purpose of the message. The correct answer is **C**. Susan's mother is offering to collect her daughter from the airport.

Reading: Part 2 matching

TIP: If you highlight or underline what each person wants, it will make it easier to find a match with similar words in the text. Remember that the information may not appear in the same order in the text.

Example

Here is an example of a Part 2 Reading task about people looking for bike rides. We have highlighted Milo's needs and the corresponding information in the text for you.

> **Q**
>
> Milo is a fit, experienced cyclist. He wants
> a difficult ride (1) that will take several hours (2), but one
> that will also provide beautiful forest scenery (3).
>
> > **East Trail**
> >
> > Waterfalls, crystal clear lakes, amazing trees (3) and forgotten river valleys all help keep the legs going on this lovely ride. It is hard (1), however, with several long steep climbs and you'll need to make sure your brakes are working for the downhill parts. You'll need three to four hours (2) to do the ride.

Explanation: East Trail is a suitable bicycle ride for Milo because it meets all of his needs. It is a 'hard' ride with steep climbs and therefore it will be 'difficult'. It goes past some 'amazing trees' and lasts 'three to four hours' so it is a ride through 'beautiful forest scenery' that takes 'several hours'.

Reading: Part 2 matching

 TIP: Be careful because there will be options that meet some of a person's needs but not all. If it does not meet **all** the needs, it is **not** the correct answer.

Example

Here is an example from a Part 2 Reading task about people looking for an e-pal. We have highlighted Dave's needs and the corresponding information in the text for you.

 Dave studies tourism and wants an e-pal with work experience in the tourist industry to help him with a college project. He wants to invite his e-pal to stay with him in future.

I have a full-time job helping my father run his own tourist apartments in the old fishing village where I live. So I'd like to improve my English without leaving home. I'm already learning English from students we employ to do summer jobs. Why not take a job with us next year? *Ali from Turkey*

Explanation: Ali only meets **one** of Dave's needs. Although he has 'experience in the tourist industry' he does not want to leave home and could not 'stay with' his e-pal in the future. He would **not** make a suitable e-pal for Dave.

Reading: Part 3 true/false

 TIP: You need to compare a question with the text to decide if it is 'true' or 'false' but you will not find the same words in both.

Examples

Here are two examples from a Part 3 Reading task. The text is about a group of people with a special interest in a music festival and the benefits they will receive. We have highlighted the key words and the corresponding information in the text for you.

 You will have the opportunity to meet the people who will play at the concerts.

You will receive invitations to private receptions where there is the chance to talk to the performers appearing at the festival.

Explanation: The question says something similar to the text: *opportunity = chance; meet = talk to; people who will play at the concerts = performers*. The overall meaning is the same and therefore the correct answer is 'true'.

 You will get details of festival events a fortnight before other people.

You will receive information about all festival concerts two weeks in advance of our general advertising to the public.

Explanation: The question says something similar to the text: *details = information; fortnight = two weeks; before = in advance of*. The overall meaning is the same and therefore the correct answer is 'true'.

Reading: Part 3 true/false

 TIP: If the information in the question does not have the same **overall** meaning as the text, the answer is 'false'.

Examples

Here are two examples from a Part 3 Reading task. The text is about a group of travellers on an organised trip to Chile. We have highlighted the key words and the corresponding information in the text for you.

 Everyone in the group will receive information about possible trips around Santiago before they arrive there.

During your free time in Santiago, members of the group can explore independently or book some extra trips. Details of these will be provided locally.

Explanation: Receiving 'information' about trips is the same as getting 'details'. But 'locally' is not the same as 'before they arrive there'. They receive the details when they are **in** Santiago so the answer is 'false'.

 The stay in San Pedro de Atacama will be busy, without any opportunities to rest during the day.

Two days are spent in the San Pedro de Atacama area, where you can visit the museum, take the Desert and Volcanoes Tour or, if you prefer, spend some time relaxing just admiring the wonderful scenery.

Explanation: The stay in San Pedro de Atacama could be 'busy' because there is a variety of trips. But the people in the group can **choose** whether they do these activities. 'Opportunities to rest' are available and therefore the correct answer is 'false'.

 *Remember that the information given in the text follows the same order as the questions.*

Reading: Part 4 multiple choice

 TIP: The first question in Part 4 is about the writer's purpose in writing the text. To help you answer the question you need to decide what the writer is doing. It helps if you know the meaning of certain verbs.

Example

Here is an example from a Part 4 Reading task. The text is about a sea captain who has become a student again at the age of 40. We have highlighted the key words and the corresponding information in the text for you.

> However, my age and greater experience also has disadvantages. My opinions are very individual and I often disagree with the teacher's views. The change from captain to student is enormous. When I was in charge of my ship, I didn't expect any arguments – and everyone respected my skills. So when an essay, which I'm proud of, gets low marks, I find it hard to accept.

 What is the writer doing in the text?

A **comparing** his views with those of other students

B **arguing** that study can help people start new careers

C **explaining** the challenges of being an older student

D **advising** students to respect the views of their teachers

Explanation: A, B, and D are wrong because the writer is not doing these things. He is not comparing his opinions with those of other students (option A) and he is not arguing that study helps with a new career (option B). Nor is he advising other students to respect their teacher's views (option D). C is the correct answer because he is explaining the challenges of being an older student.

Reading: Part 4 multiple choice

TIP: A lot of the questions in Part 4 focus on opinions and feelings, so you need to read the text carefully. If you highlight or underline the parts of the text that indicate the writer's feelings, it will help you choose the correct answer.

Example

Here is an example from a Part 4 Reading task. In the text, the writer describes her attitude towards her journey to work. We have highlighted the key words and the corresponding information in the text for you.

> For years I used to get in my car and drive to work in heavy traffic. Each day, I used to think there must be a better way of getting there. I have always loved being outdoors and I hated being stuck in the car in the middle of all that pollution. Then one day I had an idea.

 Why did the writer dislike her journey to work?

A She used to find parking difficult.

B She used to get bored on the journey.

C She didn't feel confident about driving.

D She thought she didn't get enough fresh air.

Explanation: The writer 'loved being outdoors' and she 'hated' being surrounded by pollution. The correct answer is therefore **D**.

Reading: Part 5 multiple-choice cloze

 TIP: Most of the questions in Part 5 test vocabulary but some also test grammar. You need to think carefully about the different points that are being tested.

Examples

Here are some examples of the different grammar and vocabulary points which can be tested in Part 5.

1 The four options may be similar in meaning, but only one is exactly right.

> Clara knew that if she _____ practising her piano playing would get better.
>
> **A** stayed   **B** held   **C** kept ✓   **D** remained

Explanation: The words are similar in meaning but, in this sentence, only 'kept' can be used to mean 'if she continued practising'.

2 Sometimes the answer depends on the first word after the gap.

> Antonio became _____ in photography when he was still at school.
>
> **A** fine   **B** interested ✓   **C** keen   **D** excellent

Explanation: The only word that 'interested' can be followed by is 'in'.

3 One of the four options may complete a fixed phrase such as 'get dressed'.

> If you would like to _____ part in the competition, you should see your teacher.
>
> **A** take ✓   **B** have   **C** make   **D** put

Explanation: 'Take + part + in' is a fixed phrase.

4   There may be only one correct grammatical answer.

> Becky cycled to the pool because it was _____ far to walk.
>
> **A** much   **B** even   **C** such   **D** too ✓

Explanation: 'Too + adjective' indicate that it was further than she wanted to walk.

5   One of the four options completes a phrasal verb.

> Joe had to train hard for the next race but he wasn't going to give _____ .
>
> **A** away   **B** up ✓   **C** back   **D** out

Explanation: You need a verb here that means 'to stop doing something' and only 'give + up' has this meaning.

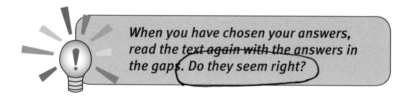

When you have chosen your answers, read the text again with the answers in the gaps. Do they seem right?

General tips for Reading

1 Remember to read the instructions for each part first. These will tell you what you need to do.

2 Answer the questions one by one. Answer the questions you are certain about first and go back to those you are unsure of later.

3 There is always information in the text to help you get the right answer – look again!

4 Always put an answer on the answer sheet even if you are not totally sure if you are correct.

5 In Part 1, try to understand the main message of the notice or short text.

6 In Part 3, read the text through quickly before looking at the questions in order to get a general understanding.

7 In Part 4, remember that the wrong answers say something similar to the text so you need to read carefully to rule them out.

 NOW YOU TRY! You will find Reading Parts 1, 2, 3, 4 and 5 to try on the CD-ROM. Give yourself 50 minutes to work through the five tasks.

When you have finished you can check your answers.

Paper 1: Reading and Writing

What's in Writing (Parts 1–3)?

Part 1 Ⓠ 5 pairs of sentences linked by theme or topic. The second sentence has a gap which you must fill using up to 3 words. The second sentence must mean exactly the same as the first.
☑ 1 mark for each correct answer

Part 2 Ⓠ 1 short message such as an email or a note to a friend (35–45 words). You are told which 3 things to write about.
☑ Total number of marks = 5

Part 3 Ⓠ 1 question from a choice of a letter to a friend or a story (approximately 100 words)
☑ Total number of marks = 15

 About **40 minutes**

In **Part 1** you are given marks for accuracy – you must write the correct answer. In **Part 2** you are given marks for successfully communicating a message – you must cover all three points. In **Part 3** you are given marks for:

- range of grammar
- range of vocabulary
- organisation of ideas
- accuracy
- register
- spelling and punctuation.

Writing: Part 1 sentence transformation

 TIP: Make sure that the second sentence, once you have filled in the gap, means the same as the first sentence.

Examples

Here are some examples (with answers) of Part 1 Writing questions.

1   The concert tickets were cheaper than Maria expected.

> The concert tickets were not as ...**expensive as**... Maria expected.

Explanation: cheaper than = not as expensive as

2   Toby's house is near the park.

> Toby's house is not ...**far from**... the park.

Explanation: near = not far from

3   Our football coach told us to train harder.

> We ...**were**... told to train harder by our football coach.

Explanation: our coach told us = we were told by our coach

4   It isn't necessary to bring mobiles on the camping trip.

> You ...**don't need**... to bring mobiles on the camping trip.

Explanation: it isn't necessary = you don't need to

Writing: Part 1 sentence transformation

 TIP: Do not write more than three words. If you do, you may lose marks.

Examples

Here are some examples (with answers) of Part 1 Writing questions.

1 Alex had not been camping before.

> This was ...**the first time**... Alex had been camping. ✓
>
> This was ...**the first time that**... Alex had been camping. ✗

Explanation: It is possible to write the sentence correctly with three words.

2 The pool is only a five-minute walk from Peter's house.

> It takes Peter five minutes ...**to walk**... to the pool. ✓
>
> It takes Peter five minutes ...**to go on foot**... to the pool. ✗

Explanation: The options mean the same but 'to go on foot' is more than three words.

3 Sara won a singing competition at the age of eight.

> Sara won a singing competition ...**when she was**... eight years old. ✓
>
> Sara won a singing competition ...**when she was only**... eight years old. ✗

Explanation: 'Only' is not necessary and adding it makes the answer more than three words.

 *Contractions count as two words, apart from 'can't' which can be written as one word 'cannot'.*

Writing: Part 2 guided writing

 TIP: Make sure you know the language for the different things you can be asked to write in a Writing Part 2 task.

Examples

Here are some examples of the things you can be asked to write in a Part 2 task. There are also examples of the language you can use.

1	make a suggestion:	Why don't we ...? Let's ...

2	give an explanation:	I can't because I have to ...

3	make an apology:	I'm really sorry but ...

4	remind somebody:	Don't forget to ... You must remember to ...

5	invite somebody:	Would you like to ...?

6	make a recommendation:	I think it's a good idea to ... I think the best thing is to ...

Remember that the word limit is 35–45 words. The more you write, the more mistakes you are likely to make and you will lose marks for writing a lot more than 45 words.

Writing: Part 2 guided writing

 TIP: It is important to write about all three of the points that are mentioned in the task. You will lose marks if you miss one out and only write about two.

Example

Here is an example of a Part 2 Writing task.

 A new sports centre has opened near your home and you would like to go there tomorrow.

Write an email to your English friend Chris. In your email you should:

• ask her to come to the sports centre with you
• explain why you want to go there
• suggest somewhere you can meet.

Write **35–45 words** on your answer sheet.

Here are two examples of student answers.

1 *Would you like to come to the new sports centre with me tomorrow afternoon?* They've got a really good pool there and we can go for a swim. *We could meet at your house if you want to go.*

2 *Do you want to go to the new sports centre tomorrow? It's only a ten-minute walk from our school. Why don't we meet outside school after the last lesson and walk to the sports centre together?*

Explanation: Example 1 is a good answer that includes all three points. In the second sentence, the writer explains why he/she wants to go to the sports centre (this is highlighted in the answer). Example 2 is not a good answer because the writer does not include this.

Writing: Part 3 extended writing (letter)

 TIP: Check your letter when you have finished, using a checklist like the one below.

Example

Here is an example of a checklist. Use it every time you practise writing a letter.

Checklist	✔
Have you written about the topic indicated in the question?	
Have you made any mistakes in spelling or grammar?	
Have you used a range of vocabulary?	
Have you written the right number of words?	
Have you written in paragraphs?	
Have you linked the points clearly?	
Have you started and ended your letter in a suitable way?	
Have you used language that is suitable for an informal letter?	

University of Cambridge ESOL Examinations

Writing: Part 3 extended writing (story)

 TIP: You can make your story more interesting by using descriptive language such as adjectives and adverbs.

Example

Here is an example of a Part 3 Writing task.

> **Your English teacher has asked you to write a story.**
>
> This is the title for your story:
>
> **A day out**
>
> Write your story on your answer sheet.

Here is an example of a student answer.

> Last Saturday, we went to a fantastic theme park and rode on some really amazing rides. I was absolutely terrified on the one called 'Wall of Death'. My cousin went on it too, but he wasn't afraid. He said he'd been on faster rides that were a lot more frightening. In the afternoon, it was very sunny and we sat on the grass eating delicious ice-creams. Then we hired a small rowing boat and spent an hour on the lake. It was a great day out – one of the best I've ever had.

Explanation: The adjectives and adverbs in the story are highlighted. They help to make the story more interesting.

General tips for Writing

1 Practise writing regularly in English, and always be aware of your reason for writing and who you are writing to.

2 Try to use new vocabulary and expressions you have learned.

3 Practise writing the same thing in different ways. This will help to make your writing more interesting.

4 Remember to plan what you write. Always think about the question and make sure that you are answering it.

5 Try to use a range of grammatical structures and tenses.

6 Read through your answers at the end to check that they are clear and that you have not made a lot of mistakes.

7 Check that your spelling and grammar are correct.

8 In **Part 3**, read the two questions carefully before making a choice. Think about whether you know enough language for the topics described and then choose.

NOW YOU TRY! You will find Writing Parts 1, 2 and 3 to try on the CD-ROM. Give yourself 40 minutes to work through the three tasks.

When you have finished you can check your answers for Part 1 and compare your answers for Part 2 (Question 6) and Part 3 (Question 7 or 8) against the sample answers.

Paper 2: Listening

What's in the Listening paper?

Part 1 ⓠ 7 short listening texts with 7 visual multiple-choice questions
☑ 1 mark for each correct answer

Part 2 ⓠ 1 long text with 6 multiple-choice questions
☑ 1 mark for each correct answer

Part 3 ⓠ 1 long monologue with 6 gap-fill questions
☑ 1 mark for each correct answer

Part 4 ⓠ 1 long dialogue with 6 true/false questions
☑ 1 mark for each correct answer

🕐 About **30 minutes**
(plus 6 minutes to copy your answers onto the answer sheet)

Listening: Part 1 multiple choice

 TIP: Use the time you have at the beginning to look at the three pictures and think about the vocabulary you may hear.

Example

Here is an example of a Part 1 Listening question.

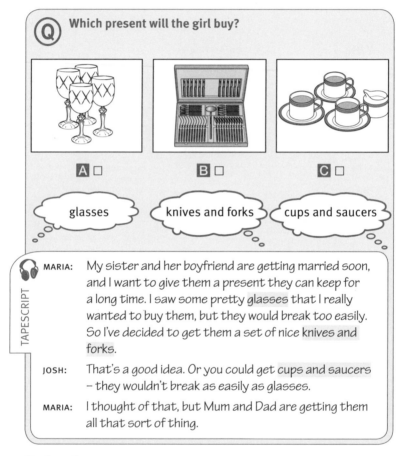

Explanation: Maria mentions 'glasses' but then says she has decided to get 'knives and forks'. Josh suggests 'cups and saucers' but Maria says that her parents are buying those. The correct answer is therefore **B**.

Listening: Part 1 multiple choice

 TIP: Read the question carefully. It may ask you to make a comparison between the three options. For example, you may have to decide what somebody liked the 'most' or the 'best'. Underline these words and think about the different ways of expressing a preference.

Example

Here is an example of a Part 1 Listening question.

Q What did the man like best about his holiday?

A ☐   B ☐   C ☐

TAPESCRIPT

I had a great holiday. The hotel room was comfortable and everything, I had nothing to complain about. It was very easy to meet people too, and I certainly had some interesting conversations. There was a great nightclub right next to the hotel – that was the most important thing because I just love dancing. The food was fine, but you know me, if it's fresh, that's all that matters.

Explanation: The man says that his room was 'comfortable', the food was 'fine' and the nightclub was 'great'. In other words, he 'liked' all of these things. However, he says that enjoying the nightclub 'was the most important thing' because he loves dancing. Therefore the correct answer is **C**.

Listening: Part 2 multiple choice

 TIP: The question may ask about the order of certain events. For example, it may ask whether option A, B or C happened 'first'. It is important to listen carefully because the correct answer may not be the first thing you hear.

Example

Here is an example from a Part 2 Listening task, which is an interview with a woman called Hilary who works as a radio disc-jockey.

 Where did Hilary <u>first</u> work as a disc-jockey?

A at a hospital

B at a university

C at a school

 HILARY: Well, I dreamed about being a disc-jockey when I was at school, but I never had the chance to try. But when I went to university, I was asked to work on student radio and that was when it all started. I really enjoyed playing music for the other students two evenings a week and I was paid for it! Several years later, I got a job in hospital radio, playing music for the patients, and after that it became my full-time job.

TAPESCRIPT

Explanation: All three places are mentioned, but **B** is the correct answer because 'it all started' at university. Hilary didn't get the 'chance' to be a disc-jockey at school and she worked in hospital radio several years after she worked on university radio.

Listening: Part 2 multiple choice

 TIP: Sometimes in multiple choice you have to complete half a sentence with one of the options. If you change the sentence into a question, it will help make it easier for you to find the correct answer.

Example

Here is an example from a Part 2 Listening task, which is an interview with a woman called Hilary who works as a radio disc-jockey.

 Hilary likes her current job because she

A talks to listeners on the phone.

B can choose the music she plays.

C prefers working in the afternoon.

INTERVIEWER: *And do you enjoy your current job on national radio?*

HILARY: *Yes, it's an afternoon show, which is nice but I'd really prefer to work in the evening when there's a younger audience. The good thing is that nobody tells me what music to put on – so I can play all my favourites. In my last job, I used to talk to listeners on the phone, which I didn't really like.*

Explanation: The question here is 'Why does Hilary like her current job?' The answer is not C because she would 'prefer to work in the evening'. Neither is the answer A because she didn't like talking to people on the phone. The correct answer is **B** because she says 'the good thing is that nobody tells me what music to put on'.

Listening: Part 3 gap-fill

 TIP: You need to read the questions carefully and think about the kind of information that is missing, for example, is it a noun? Is it a number? This will help you decide what you need to listen for.

Example

Here is an example from a Part 3 Listening task in which a radio presenter is giving some information for visitors to a national park.

BRIDGEWATER NATIONAL PARK

(Q) **Accommodation: (1)** _____ **in the forest and guest houses near the lake.**

TAPESCRIPT

If you would like to stay for a few days, the national park offers different kinds of accommodation. Camping is not allowed so you don't need to take a tent with you. But there are cabins in the woods that visitors can stay in overnight. These sleep up to four people and have cooking facilities. There are also some larger guest houses by the lake that up to six people can stay in.

Explanation: You know from reading the question paper that you are listening for a noun to describe a type of accommodation. You 'don't need to take a tent' and 'guest houses' is already on the question paper, so the correct answer is 'cabins'.

 *Write only the missing word or short phrase on the answer sheet in Part 3, and don't rephrase it.*

Listening: Part 3 gap-fill

 TIP: There are usually one or more questions about times, dates and prices in a Part 3 Listening task. You will hear different numbers that **could** fit in the gaps, but only one of them is correct. Listen carefully to the language around the numbers to decide on the correct answer.

Example
Here is an example from a Part 3 task in which a sports instructor is giving information about windsurfing lessons.

 Times of windsurfing lessons
Lessons for beginners: 08.30 – 09.30
Advanced lessons: 09.45 – **(1)** _____

As usual the beginners' windsurfing classes start at 08.30. They finish at 09.30 and they're followed by lessons for more advanced students at 09.45. The advanced classes used to start immediately after the beginners' but the trainer needed a break between classes so we moved the advanced class to 09.45. The advanced class is still an hour long and it now finishes at 10.45 instead of 10.30.

Explanation: 08.30 and 09.30 are the times of the beginners' lessons and these are already on the question paper. The advanced class used to finish at 10.30 but now it finishes at 10.45. The correct answer is therefore 10.45.

Listening: Part 4 true/false

 TIP: Most of the questions in this task focus on a speaker's attitude or feelings. It is helpful to highlight or underline the words in the question that are connected with opinions or feelings so that you know what to listen for.

Example
Here is an example from a Part 4 Listening task in which two friends, Jake and Sam, are talking about sport. Is this statement 'true' or 'false'?

 Jake was <u>disappointed</u> with last Saturday's football match.

TAPESCRIPT

JAKE: It was really difficult to get tickets for last Saturday's match and I was looking forward to it all week. We didn't have the best seats but I didn't mind. The last game I'd seen at the stadium was really boring but not this one. It was a great game. It's a shame you missed it

Explanation: Although Jake was disappointed with the last match at the stadium and he also had problems getting tickets, he says that last Saturday's match was 'a great game'. He was not 'disappointed' and therefore the answer is 'false'.

Listening: Part 4 true/false

 TIP: There is often a question about whether the two speakers agree or not. If you highlight or underline the opinion in the question, you can then listen carefully to find out whether the second speaker agrees with the first. The agreement may come at the end of the second speaker's turn, so do not make a decision too quickly.

Example

Here is an example from a Part 4 Listening task in which two university students, Neil and Alicia, are talking about Neil's new flat.

 Neil agrees that living alone can be difficult.

TAPESCRIPT

ALICIA: You're not going to feel lonely, are you? Living on your own can be quite hard at first.

NEIL: I did wonder about that. There were nearly always people around me at home. But I really enjoyed it when my parents went away last summer and I was by myself. I worked better and I really enjoyed the peace. No, I'm going to be fine.

Explanation: Alicia believes that 'living on your own can be quite hard' but Neil doesn't agree. He expresses some doubt at first but then says he enjoyed himself when he was alone last summer and he thinks that he's 'going to be fine'. Therefore the answer is 'false'.

General tips for Listening

1 Use the time you are given to read through the questions so that you know exactly what you are listening for.

2 You hear the instructions on the recording. Always listen carefully and read the question at the same time, as the instructions and question give you the context and the topic.

3 If you are not sure, choose the answer that you think is probably right.

4 Use the second listening to check your answer even if you are sure you are right. Don't stop listening!

5 Make sure you write clearly when copying your answers onto the answer sheet. You have plenty of time to do this.

6 Remember that in **Parts 2, 3** and **4** the questions are in the same order as the recording.

 NOW YOU TRY! You will find a complete Listening paper to try on the CD-ROM, as well as all the recordings you need. You have about 35 minutes to work through the whole paper.

When you have finished you can check your answers.

 *On the first listening, don't worry if you have not got all the answers. Only fill in the answers you are sure of, and use the second listening to check your ideas for the other answers.*

Paper 3: Speaking

What's in the Speaking test?

Part 1 (Q) You answer the examiner's questions about yourself and give your opinions.

Part 2 (Q) You talk about a situation with your partner. There is a page of pictures to help you.

Part 3 (Q) You describe a photograph on your own. (Your partner will talk about a different photograph on the same topic.)

Part 4 (Q) You tell your partner what you think about a topic and find out what he or she thinks about it.

(⏱) **10–12 minutes** *per pair of candidates*

Your speaking is assessed on:

- grammar and vocabulary
- discourse management
- pronunciation
- interactive communication
- global achievement.

Speaking: Part 1 interview

 TIP: The examiner asks you for your name and other personal details, then asks you more general questions about yourself. Make your answers interesting by giving reasons for what you say and keep talking until the examiner tells you to stop.

Examples

Here are some examples of questions and answers from candidates in Speaking Part 1.

1

EXAMINER:	What do you enjoy doing in your free time?
CANDIDATE:	I like to spend time with my friends. Sometimes we go to the cinema, but usually they come to my house because it's near our school. We usually listen to music or play computer games. But they don't stay very long. We have a lot of homework to do. That's why we don't spend more time together.

2

EXAMINER:	Do you think that English will be useful for you in the future?
CANDIDATE:	Yes, I think English will be useful for me in the future. Nearly everyone in my country studies English because it's an international language. You need English for all kinds of work and I'm studying English so that I can get a good job in the future.

Explanation: In examples 1 and 2 the candidates give reasons. Look at the highlighted words.

3

EXAMINER:	Do you enjoy studying English?
CANDIDATE:	Yes. I usually enjoy it, but not all the time. I like talking to my friends in English and we have a really good teacher. Some things that we study, like the different tenses, are quite difficult and I don't like that so much. But it's fun when we can listen to English songs and understand the words.

4

EXAMINER:	What did you do last weekend?
CANDIDATE:	It was just a normal weekend really. I'm a member of a swimming club and on Saturday I went to my swimming lesson. After that I met my friends and we went shopping together. On Sunday I spent most of the day with my family. We went to visit my grandparents and we stayed there most of the afternoon and had dinner with them.

Explanation: In examples 3 and 4 the candidates keep talking by adding more information in their answers.

Speaking: Part 2 collaborative task

TIP: Talk about all the ideas in the pictures first, and then at the end you can decide which is the best idea. Say why each picture is a good idea or a bad idea and give your reasons. Don't choose the best idea too quickly because you need to keep talking for 2–3 minutes.

Example

Here is an example of a Part 2 task. The picture is on pages 48–9.

> **EXAMINER:** **I'm going to describe a situation to you. A student is visiting Britain and wants to take a present home for her 13-year-old brother. Talk together about the different things she could buy and decide which would be best. Here is a picture with some ideas to help you.**
>
> CANDIDATE A: What would be a good present for a 13-year-old? Let's talk about all the pictures first.
>
> CANDIDATE B: OK. I think the teddy bear and the doll, the picture here, is too young for him. What about you?
>
> CANDIDATE A: You're right. And what about the cakes and chocolate? I'm not sure about them. I don't think they're a very exciting present if you're thirteen.
>
> CANDIDATE B: No, I agree with you. Perhaps these games then – the puzzle and the electronic game. Do you think he'd like those?
>
> CANDIDATE A: I think so – but he's probably got something like that already. How about the T-shirt and the cap?
>
> CANDIDATE B: Perhaps, but I'm sure he'd like these football things more. Most 13-year-old boys like football.
>
> CANDIDATE A: Shall we choose the football things then? There's one other thing here. What do you think about the CD?
>
> CANDIDATE B: I think he probably downloads all his music. So, let's go for the football things?
>
> CANDIDATE A: OK. I think that's the best present.

Explanation: The example shows two good candidates discussing all the different ideas and then choosing the best one.

Speaking: Part 2 collaborative task

 TIP: Remember to say what you think about the ideas and to ask for your partner's opinion as well.

Example

Here is an example of a Part 2 task. The picture is on pages 48–9.

> EXAMINER: **I'm going to describe a situation to you. A student is visiting Britain and wants to take a present home for her 13-year-old brother. Talk together about the different things she could buy and decide which would be best. Here is a picture with some ideas to help you.**

> CANDIDATE A: What would be a good present for a 13-year-old? Let's talk about all the pictures first.
>
> CANDIDATE B: OK. I think the teddy bear and the doll, the picture here, is too young for him. What about you?
>
> CANDIDATE A: You're right. And what about the cakes and chocolate? I'm not sure about them. I don't think they're a very exciting present if you're 13.
>
> CANDIDATE B: No, I agree with you. Perhaps these games then – the puzzle and the electronic game. Do you think he'd like those?
>
> CANDIDATE A: I think so – but he's probably got something like that already. How about the T-shirt and the cap?
>
> CANDIDATE B: Perhaps, but I'm sure he'd like these football things more. Most thirteen-year-old boys like football.
>
> CANDIDATE A: Shall we choose the football things then? There's one other thing here. What do you think about the CD?
>
> CANDIDATE B: I think he probably downloads all his music. So, let's go for the football things?
>
> CANDIDATE A: OK. I think that's the best present.

Explanation: The highlighted words are ways of giving your opinion and asking for your partner's opinion.

Remember that the examiner repeats the instructions in Part 2, so don't worry if you don't understand them the first time.

Speaking: Part 3 long turn

 TIP: You need to describe everything you can see in the photograph. You can talk about the people, what they are doing and what they are wearing. You should also describe the place and the things you can see there.

Example

Here is an example of a Part 3 Speaking task. You can find the photo on page 52. You may be the first candidate to describe a photo (Candidate A) or the second (Candidate B). The examiner will tell you what the photos are about and will give each of you a different photo about the same topic.

> CANDIDATE: I can see six students in the picture. They look about 18 or 19 years old and they are all wearing T-shirts and I think it's summer time. They're all sitting around a big table. There are lots of books on the table and also some files. The students are studying together and helping each other. They probably all study at the same college and they are doing their homework together. I think that they are in a library because there are lots of shelves behind them. Maybe it is the library in the college where they study.
>
> The boy on the right has a pen in his hand and he's pointing at something in a book. He's showing the book to the others. Maybe he's trying to explain something to them. All the others are looking at him and they are listening to what he's saying. Except for the girl in the red T-shirt, she seems to be a bit bored. She's got a pen in her hand but she isn't writing anything.

Explanation: The candidate uses the highlighted words to describe the place, the people and what they are doing.

Speaking: Part 3 long turn

 TIP: As well as describing what you can see in the photograph, you should also say what you think is true.

Example

Here is an example of a Part 3 Speaking task. You can find the photo on page 52.

> CANDIDATE: I can see six students in the picture. They look about 18 or 19 years old and they are all wearing T-shirts and I think it's summer time. They're all sitting around a big table. There are lots of books on the table and also some files. The students are studying together and helping each other. They probably all study at the same college and they are doing their homework together. I think they are in a library because there are lots of shelves behind them. Maybe it is the library in the college where they study.
>
> The boy on the right has a pen in his hand and he's pointing at something in a book. He's showing the book to the others. Maybe he's trying to explain something to them. All the others are looking at him and they are listening to what he's saying. Except for the girl in the red T-shirt, she seems to be a bit bored. She's got a pen in her hand but she isn't writing anything.

Explanation: The candidate uses the highlighted words to say what he/she thinks is true.

Speaking: Part 4 discussion

 TIP: In this part you should have a normal conversation with your partner. You can say what you think, but you also need to find out what your partner thinks. It is important to ask for your partner's opinions and to react to what he or she says.

Example

Here is an example of a discussion from a Part 4 Speaking task.

EXAMINER:	**Your photographs showed people studying in different places. Now, I'd like you to talk together about where you like to study and the best time of day for studying.**
CANDIDATE A:	Well, I prefer studying somewhere on my own because I don't like studying in a group. I think a quiet place, like my room, is good. What about you? Do you think it's best to study alone?
CANDIDATE B:	I'm not sure. I think you can learn in groups too because other people can help you if you don't understand something.
CANDIDATE A:	I suppose so. But I still prefer to work alone in my room.
CANDIDATE B:	I agree that your own room is a good place to study but I also like studying in places like the library where you can work with your friends. One thing I don't like is studying when there's really loud music on.
CANDIDATE A:	Me too. That's terrible – especially my brother's music! And what about the time of day? Do you prefer the morning or the evening?
CANDIDATE B:	I think the morning is the best time to study because you can get more done then. In the evening you need to chill out!

> **CANDIDATE A:** *Oh, I don't agree.* I find it easier to work in the evening. It takes me a long time to wake up in the morning.
>
> **CANDIDATE B:** *Well, everyone's different.*

Explanation: The candidates use the highlighted words to show different ways of giving opinions and having a conversation with your partner.

Remember that there are no right or wrong opinions. It is the language you use that matters.

General tips for Speaking

1 Listen to the examiner's instructions carefully and ask if you don't understand.

2 Always speak clearly so that the examiners can hear you.

3 Don't worry if you make a grammatical mistake – you can still get a good mark if you make mistakes.

4 Try to have a normal conversation. React to what the examiner and your partner says to you.

5 Don't worry if the examiner stops you before you have finished everything that you want to say. It's because the test is carefully timed.

6 Say what you think, but give your partner time to talk too and show interest in what your partner says.

7 Relax and try not to be nervous – enjoy the experience!

 NOW YOU TRY! You will find video of a complete Speaking test on the CD-ROM, together with the pictures and the script for the examiner. Practise with a partner, and you will feel more confident when you take the test.

What to do on the day

Very few people like taking exams, but you can make the day of the exam easier if you make sure you know what to expect and what you will have to do before you go to the exam centre or place where you take your PET exam.

Rules and regulations

For any exam you take, there are some rules and regulations about what you must do and what you mustn't do during the exam. Read through the Cambridge ESOL rules and regulations below and if there is anything you don't understand, ask your teacher. On the day of the exam, you can also ask the examination supervisor if you are not sure.

You must ...
- provide a valid photographic proof of your identity (for example: national identity card, passport, college ID or driving licence) and your Statement of Entry for each paper you take.
- only have on your desk what you need to complete the examination (pens, pencils and erasers).
- switch off your mobile phone and any other electronic device. The supervisor will tell you where you have to put them.
- stop writing immediately when you are told to do so.

You must not ...
- cheat, copy, give anything to another candidate, take anything from another candidate, or break any of the rules during the examination.
- have with you any electronic device. This includes mobile phones.
- use, or attempt to use, a dictionary.
- use correction fluid on the answer sheets.
- talk to or disturb other candidates during the examination.
- smoke or eat in the examination room. However, you are allowed to drink plain, still water from a plastic bottle with a secure lid.

Advice and information

We hope that all our candidates will have a positive experience
of taking a Cambridge ESOL exam. So, we have prepared some
advice and information so that you know what to do if there are any
problems on the day that you take your exam. Make sure that you
have read and understand all the information and advice below
before you go into the exam.

Make sure you are on time

- Know the date, time and place of your examination and arrive
  well before the start time.
- If you arrive late for any part of the examination, report to the
  supervisor or invigilator. You may not be allowed to take the
  examination. Also, if you are admitted, not all of your work may
  be accepted.
- If you miss any part of the examination, you will not normally be
  given a grade.

Instructions for taking the test

- The supervisor will tell you what you have to do. The
  instructions are also written on the question paper and the
  answer sheet.
- Listen to the supervisor and read the instructions carefully.
- Tell the supervisor or invigilator at once if you think you have the
  wrong question paper, or if the question paper is incomplete or
  badly printed.

Advice and assistance during the examination

- If you are not sure about what to do, raise your hand to attract
  attention. The invigilator will come to help you.
- You must not ask for, and will not be given, any explanation of
  the questions.
- If you do not feel well on the day of the examination or think
  that your work may be affected for any other reason, tell the
  supervisor or invigilator.

Leaving the examination room

- Do not leave the examination room for any reason without the permission of the supervisor or invigilator.
- The supervisor will tell you when you can and can't leave the room.
- You must wait until the supervisor has collected your question paper, answer sheet(s) and any paper used for rough work before you leave the examination room.
- You must not take any information relating to the examination questions or answers out of the examination room.
- Do not make any noise near the examination room.

Answer sheets (for the paper and pencil test)

On the day you take the exam, you can write on the question paper while you decide what the correct answer is. However, when you have made a decision, you must transfer your final answers onto the candidate answer sheets which the supervisor will give you for the Reading and Writing and Listening papers.

How to complete the answer sheets

You can see an example of what an answer sheet looks like on the next page. There are instructions on the answer sheets to tell you how you should fill them in, but here are the main things you need to know:

- It is very important that you use a pencil to write your answers on the answer sheets. (We use a special machine to check some of your answers and it can only 'see' pencil marks.)
- Where you have to choose an answer (A, B, C or D, etc.), you must make a clear pencil mark inside the box you choose. Don't, for example, put a circle around the box, because the machine won't 'see' this.
- If you have to write a word or phrase for your answer, please write clearly. If the examiners can't read your writing, they won't know if your answer is correct or not.
- If you change your mind about an answer, it is important that you use an eraser to rub out the answer you don't want.

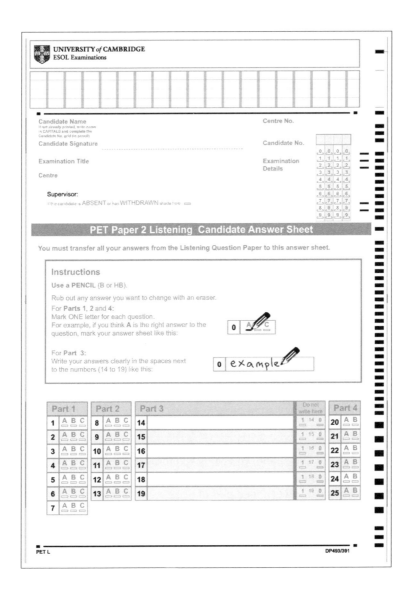

UNIVERSITY *of* CAMBRIDGE
ESOL Examinations

Candidate Name
If not already printed, write name in CAPITALS and complete the Candidate No. grid (in pencil)

Candidate Signature

Examination Title

Centre

Supervisor:
If the candidate is ABSENT or has WITHDRAWN shade here

Centre No.

Candidate No.

Examination Details

0	0	0	0
1	1	1	1
2	2	2	2
3	3	3	3
4	4	4	4
5	5	5	5
6	6	6	6
7	7	7	7
8	8	8	8
9	9	9	9

PET Paper 2 Listening Candidate Answer Sheet

You must transfer all your answers from the Listening Question Paper to this answer sheet.

Instructions

Use a **PENCIL** (B or HB).

Rub out any answer you want to change with an eraser.

For **Parts 1**, **2** and **4**:
Mark ONE letter for each question.
For example, if you think **A** is the right answer to the question, mark your answer sheet like this:

0 A B C

For **Part 3**:
Write your answers clearly in the spaces next to the numbers (14 to 19) like this:

0 example

Part 1		Part 2		Part 3		Do not write here	Part 4	
1	A B C	8	A B C	14		1 14 0	20	A B
2	A B C	9	A B C	15		1 15 0	21	A B
3	A B C	10	A B C	16		1 16 0	22	A B
4	A B C	11	A B C	17		1 17 0	23	A B
5	A B C	12	A B C	18		1 18 0	24	A B
6	A B C	13	A B C	19		1 19 0	25	A B
7	A B C							

PET L

DP493/391

Computer-based PET (CB PET)

There is a computer-based exam for PET that leads to the internationally recognised Cambridge ESOL certificate. This computer version of PET is available to centres with the appropriate equipment and training. The tasks are exactly the same as for the paper and pencil test. The only thing that is different is that you take the Reading and Writing, and the Listening papers on a computer.

If you prefer to take the test on a computer, there are other aspects of CB PET that may be an advantage:
- You can take CB PET at a range of different times in the year.
- You can register for the exam as little as two weeks before taking it.
- Your results are available online just three weeks after you take the test.

When you are taking the exam, there are certain features of the CB test that will help you:
- There is a tutorial that you can watch before taking the test, which gives you advice on how to complete your answers.
- You can edit your answers on screen during the exam, so if you decide to change something it is easy to do so.
- There is a clock on screen which shows you how much time you have left.
- On the Reading paper you can scroll through the longer texts. You can also go backwards and forwards through the sections. This means you can read part of a text again if you want to check something.
- You write your answers on screen for the Writing paper. There is a word counter, which shows you how many words you have written.
- You are able to use headphones during the Listening paper, so you can adjust the volume if you need to.

- Remember that the Speaking paper for CB PET is carried out in the same way as the paper and pencil exam.

If you are interested in doing CB PET, you should contact your exam centre to find out more.

NOTE: The PET exam on the *Top Tips for PET* CD-ROM looks like a CB PET exam, but the real CB PET exam does not include all the same features.

What next after PET?

We hope that you will enjoy studying for PET and that you will be successful when you take the exam. A Cambridge ESOL qualification is a great achievement and you can be proud of your result.

When you receive your results and certificate, you will probably start to think about what you can do next to continue to improve your English, so here are some suggestions.

Using PET for work or study
Many companies and educational institutions in different countries recognise PET as proof of your level of English when you are looking for a job or applying for a place to study.

For the future, you may be thinking about studying abroad or working in a company where you need to use your English. If this is something which interests you, have a look at the Recognition database on the Cambridge ESOL website:

www.CambridgeESOL.org/recognition

Search the database for the specific information you need about how and where you can use PET. Using the information in the database, you can find out about the many possibilities, both for work and further study, which are open to you when you pass PET.

Taking the next Cambridge ESOL exam
If you are thinking of continuing your English studies, the next level of the Cambridge ESOL exams for you is the First Certificate in English (FCE). You can find more information about FCE on our Candidate Support website at:

www.candidates.CambridgeESOL.org

Installing your *Top Tips for PET* CD-ROM

Please set your screen resolution to 800 x 600 to get the best out of your *Top Tips for PET* CD-ROM.

For Microsoft Windows

(1) Insert the *Top Tips for PET* CD-ROM into your CD-ROM drive. If you have Autorun enabled, Windows will automatically launch the Installation wizard for installing *Top Tips for PET*. If not, double click the Top_Tips_for_PET.exe from the CD-ROM.

Top_Tips_for_PET.exe

(2) Follow the Installation wizard steps.
(3) After the installation completes, you can access the application from the Start menu.
(4) You can also launch the application by double clicking the shortcut on the Desktop.
(5) To uninstall the application, click Uninstall Top Tips for PET from the Start menu.

For Mac OS X (10.3 or later)

Top Tips for PET is distributed as a package ('.pkg') file for Mac OS X:

(1) Insert the *Top Tips for PET* CD-ROM into your CD-ROM drive. The *Top Tips for PET* icon will appear on your Desktop.
(2) Double click the icon. Mac OS X will display the contents of the CD-ROM.
(3) Double click the file 'Top Tips for PET.pkg'. This will launch the Installer.

(4) Simply click Continue on the Installer's Welcome screen to proceed with the installation.

(5) Just before the Installer copies the files, you will need to enter the administrator's password.

(6) After the installation is completed, the Top Tips for PET application will reside as a folder named *Top Tips for PET* inside the Applications folder.

(7) Double click the Top Tips for PET folder to view its contents.

(8) Then double click the Top Tips for PET file to launch *Top Tips for PET*.

(9) NOTE: To easily open *Top Tips for PET*, you can drag it to the dock.

(10) To uninstall the application move the Top Tips for PET folder from the Applications folder to the Trash.

System requirements

For PC

Essential:	Windows 2000, XP or Vista, CD drive and audio capabilities
Recommended:	400 MHz processor or faster, with 256mb of RAM or more

For Mac

Essential:	Mac OS X, version 10.3 or higher
Recommended:	400 MHz G3 processor or faster, with 256mb of RAM or more